A Picture Book of
Rosa Parks

David A. Adler

illustrated by Robert Casilla

Holiday House/New York

Library of Congress Cataloging-in-Publication Data
Adler, David A.
A picture book of Rosa Parks / David A. Adler ; illustrated by
Robert Casilla.—1st ed.
p.   cm.
Summary: A biography of the Alabama black woman whose refusal to
give up her seat on a bus helped establish the civil rights
movement.
ISBN 0-8234-1041-2
1. Parks, Rosa, 1913-   —Juvenile literature. 2. Afro-Americans—
Alabama—Montgomery—Biography—Juvenile literature. 3. Civil
rights workers—Alabama—Montgomery—Biography—Juvenile literature.
4. Montgomery (Ala.)—Biography—Juvenile literature. 5. Afro-
Americans—Civil rights—Alabama—Montgomery—Juvenile literature.
6. Segregation in transportation—Alabama—Montgomery—Juvenile
literature. 7. Montgomery (Ala.)—Race relations—Juvenile
literature. [1. Parks, Rosa, 1913-   . 2. Afro-Americans—
Biography. 3. Afro-Americans—Civil rights.]   I. Casilla, Robert,
ill. II. Title.
F334.M753P3823   1993   92-41826   CIP   AC
323'.092—dc20
[B]
ISBN 0-8234-1177-X (pbk.)

Other books in David A. Adler's *Picture Book Biography* series

Rosa Parks was born in Tuskegee, Alabama, on February 4, 1913. Her mother, Leona Edwards McCauley, was a schoolteacher. Rosa's father, James McCauley, was a carpenter and housebuilder. Rosa was the great-granddaughter of slaves.

Soon after Rosa was born, her family moved to Pine Level, Alabama. They lived on Rosa's grandparents' small farm where there were cows, chickens, fruit, and nut trees.

In 1915, when Rosa was two years old, her brother Sylvester was born. Soon after that their father left. He moved around to find work. While Rosa was growing up, she hardly saw him.

As Rosa grew older, she worked on her grandparents' farm and in the nearby cotton fields. In the spring she cleared weeds away. In the fall she picked cotton.

While Rosa lived in Pine Level, the Ku Klux Klan, a band of hate-filled whites, was active there. They wore white robes and covered their faces with pointed hoods. In southern cities and elsewhere in the United States, members of the Klan marched and helped elect political candidates who shared their hatred of African Americans, Roman Catholics, Jews, and foreigners. They burned crosses and beat, tortured, and killed many African Americans. Rosa's grandfather, Sylvester Edwards, carried a shotgun to protect his family from the Klan.

·WHITE·

When Rosa was young, discrimination against African Americans was common. There were "Jim Crow" laws that kept black people and white people segregated. They were kept apart on streetcars and trains, at parks and drinking fountains, in churches, hotels, theaters, and restaurants. Even the United States Army was segregated.

Rosa's mother taught Rosa to read. Then, when Rosa was six years old, she started first grade in an old one-room school for African American children. The school was open just five months a year. The new brick school building for white children was open nine months a year.

School for black children in Pine Level stopped after sixth grade, so in 1924 Rosa continued her studies in Montgomery, Alabama. She had to leave school in 1929 because of family illness. She took care of her sick grandmother, and then she cared for her mother who was sick, too. Rosa finished high school in 1933.

In 1931 Rosa met Raymond Parks, a barber and a man active in the struggle for the rights of African Americans. Rosa was proud that he spoke up for what was right. Rosa and Raymond were married in December 1932 in her mother's home in Pine Level.

In the early 1940s, Rosa joined the NAACP, the National Association for the Advancement of Colored People, an organization that worked to end the unfair treatment of African Americans and others. Raymond Parks had been a member for many years. Soon after Rosa joined, she was elected secretary of the Montgomery branch of the association.

Buses in Montgomery were a daily reminder that the city was segregated. African Americans were allowed only to sit in the back. On some buses they entered through the front door, paid the fare, and were told to leave the bus and go in again through the back door. Sometimes, before they could get on again, the driver drove away.

One day in 1943, Rosa got on the front of a crowded bus and paid the fare. The driver, James Blake, told her to get off and use the back door. Rosa told him she was already on the bus. She didn't see the need to get off, and besides that, she didn't think she could enter through the back door. It was blocked by the many people standing there. But Rosa got off. She didn't get on again. She waited for the next bus.

Twelve years later, on Thursday December 1, 1955, Rosa Parks met James Blake again. Rosa was coming home from her work as a tailor's assistant at a Montgomery department store. She got on the Cleveland Avenue bus and took a seat in the middle section. African Americans were allowed to sit in the back and in the middle section, too, as long as no white passenger was left standing.

At the next stop, some white passengers got on, and, because the bus was crowded, moved to the middle section, where Rosa was sitting. The driver told the four African American passengers in Rosa's row to get up. Three of them did, but not Rosa Parks. She had paid the same fare as the white passengers. She knew it was the law in Montgomery that she give up her seat, but she also knew the law was unfair. James Blake called the police, and Rosa Parks was arrested.

On Monday, December 5, Rosa went to the local court and was found guilty of breaking the segregation laws. She was fined ten dollars plus court costs. Rosa and her lawyers appealed to a higher court.

Beginning on December 5, to protest the arrest of Rosa Parks, African Americans in Montgomery refused to ride on public buses. They found other ways to get to work. Many walked, some as far as twelve miles.

The bus boycott was led by Dr. Martin Luther King, Jr., the new minister at the Dexter Avenue Baptist Church. On Monday evening, December 5, he spoke to a large crowd. He explained the reason for the boycott. "There comes a time," he said, "that people get tired. We are here this evening to say to those who have mistreated us so long, that we are tired—tired of being segregated and humiliated, tired of being kicked about by the brutal feet of oppression."

The boycott lasted more than a year. During that time almost no African Americans rode a public bus in Montgomery, Alabama.

Rosa Parks, Dr. King, and many others were arrested. Homes of boycott leaders were bombed.

On November 13, 1956, the United States Supreme Court ruled that segregation on public buses was against the law. On December 21, after the court order reached Montgomery, the boycott ended. News reporters came to talk to Rosa and to photograph her sitting on a bus again.

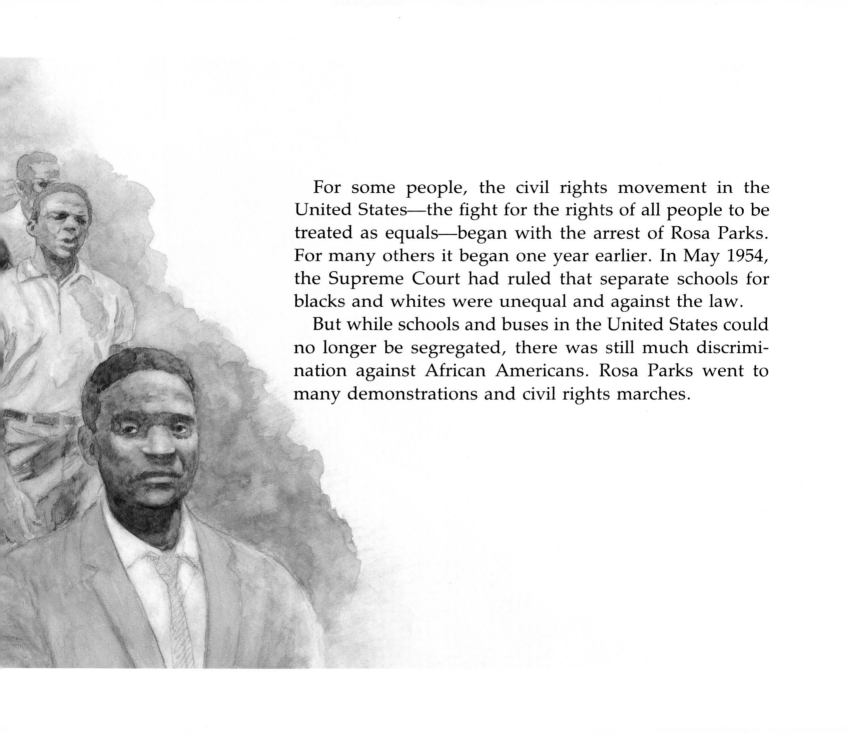

For some people, the civil rights movement in the United States—the fight for the rights of all people to be treated as equals—began with the arrest of Rosa Parks. For many others it began one year earlier. In May 1954, the Supreme Court had ruled that separate schools for blacks and whites were unequal and against the law.

But while schools and buses in the United States could no longer be segregated, there was still much discrimination against African Americans. Rosa Parks went to many demonstrations and civil rights marches.

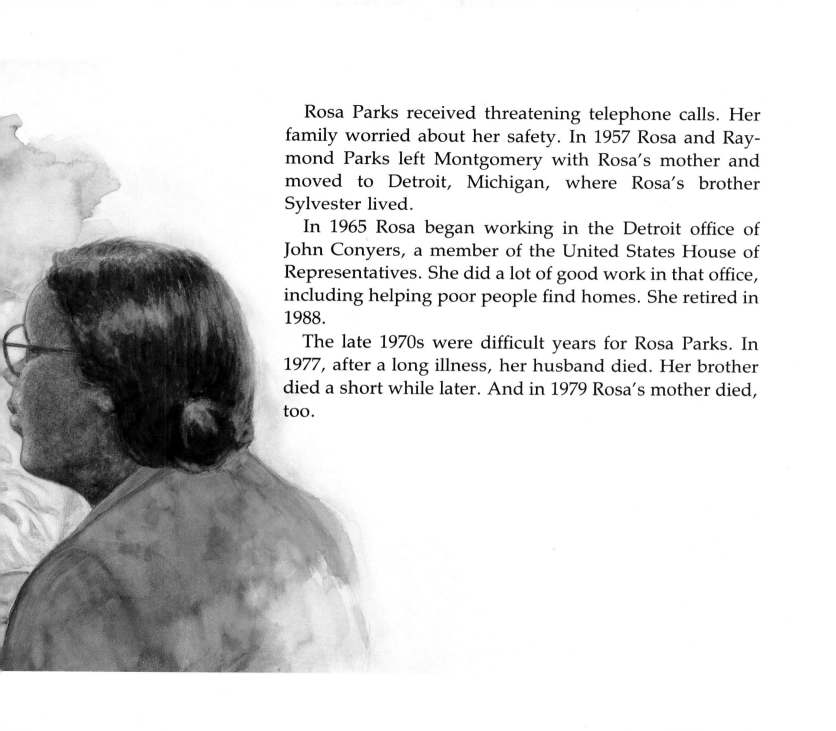

Rosa Parks received threatening telephone calls. Her family worried about her safety. In 1957 Rosa and Raymond Parks left Montgomery with Rosa's mother and moved to Detroit, Michigan, where Rosa's brother Sylvester lived.

In 1965 Rosa began working in the Detroit office of John Conyers, a member of the United States House of Representatives. She did a lot of good work in that office, including helping poor people find homes. She retired in 1988.

The late 1970s were difficult years for Rosa Parks. In 1977, after a long illness, her husband died. Her brother died a short while later. And in 1979 Rosa's mother died, too.

In 1987 Rosa founded the Rosa and Raymond Parks Institute for Self-Development to give young people hope and to help them complete their education.

Rosa Parks has been called the "Mother of the Civil Rights Movement." The movement brought many needed changes in the United States. It is now against the law for Americans to discriminate against people because of their race, color, religion, or nationality, at work or in restaurants, hotels, and other public places. The right of every citizen to vote is protected.

Rosa Parks has received many honors, among them the Spingarn Medal, the Martin Luther King, Jr., Nonviolent Peace Prize, the Eleanor Roosevelt Woman of Courage Award, and the Presidential Medal of Freedom. Cleveland Avenue in Montgomery was renamed Rosa Parks Boulevard.

But perhaps the greatest reward for Rosa Parks is seeing people of all races on buses and in public schools and other places being treated fairly and with the respect all people deserve.

AUTHOR'S NOTES

Tuskegee, Alabama, Rosa Parks's birthplace, was the home of the Tuskegee Institute, now called Tuskegee University. It was founded in 1881 by Booker T. Washington (1856–1915) as a place for African Americans to learn the work skills needed to earn a livelihood.

The lawyer presenting the arguments against segregated schools which led to the 1954 Supreme Court decision declaring that separate schools for whites and African Americans are illegal, was Thurgood Marshall. In 1967 he was made the first African American associate justice of the United States Supreme Court.

IMPORTANT DATES

1913   Born in Tuskegee, Alabama, on February 4.

1932   Married Raymond Parks.

1943   Elected secretary of the Montgomery chapter of the NAACP.

1954   The Supreme Court ruled on May 17 in *Brown* v. *Board of Education of Topeka* that segregated schools are unequal and violate the Constitution of the United States.

1955   Arrested on December 1 for not moving to the back of the bus.

1955   The Montgomery bus boycott began on December 5. It ended December 21, 1956.

1956   Supreme Court declared on November 13 that segregation on public buses violates the Constitution of the United States.

1957   Moved to Detroit, Michigan.

1965   Began work for Congressman John Conyers.

1987   Founded the Rosa and Raymond Parks Institute for Self-Development.
         Was awarded the Medal of Freedom.